Australia

Distant Encounters

Stephen and Scharlie Platt

Australia: Distant Encounters
First published - August 2017
Published by
Leveret Publishing
56 Covent Garden, Cambridge, CB1 2HR, UK

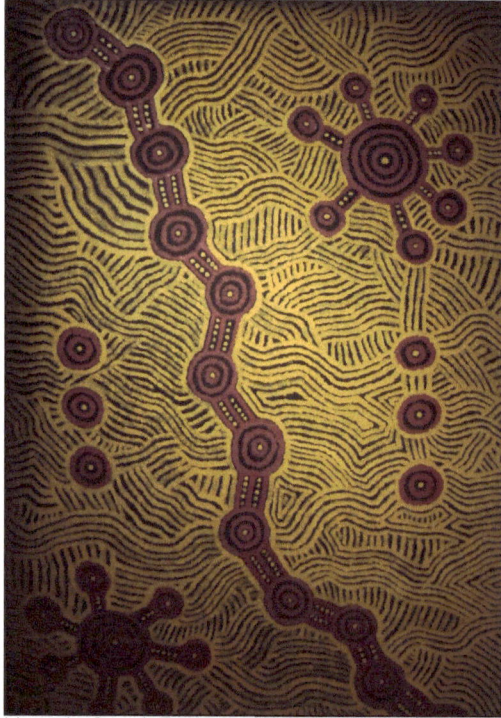

Nyaru by Brandy Tjungurrayi, Warlayirti Artists, 2007.

ISBN 978-0-9957680-5-5

Australia
Distant Encounters

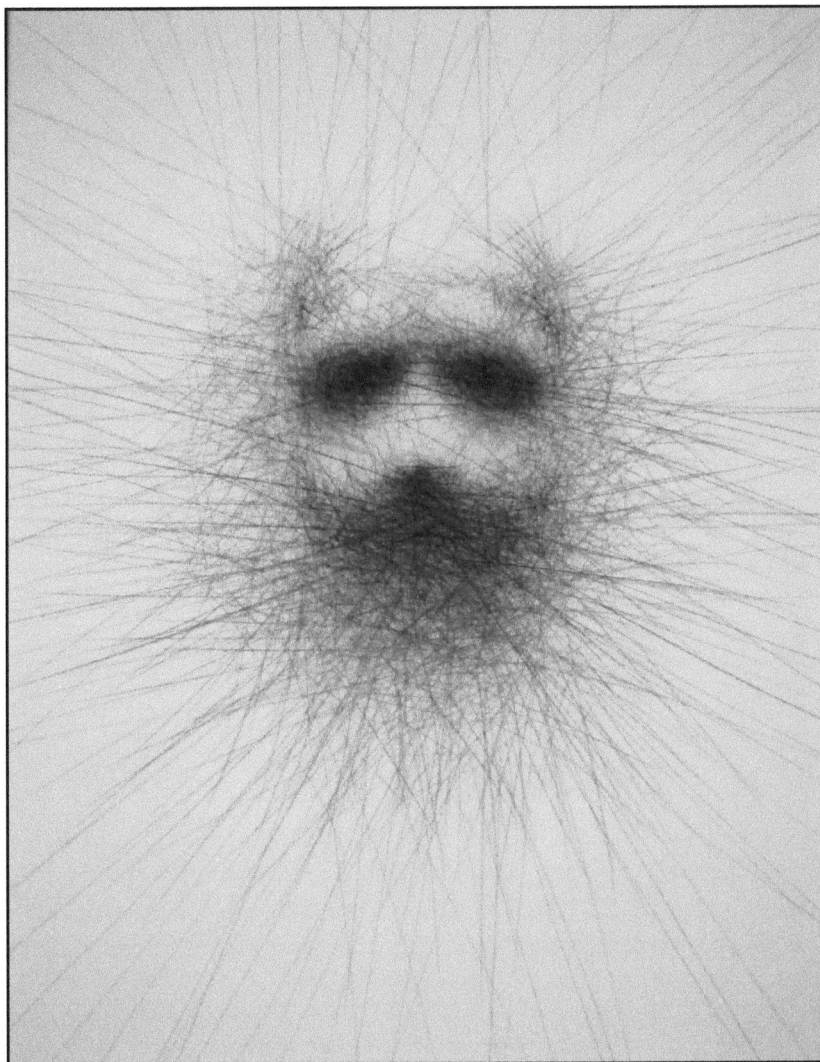

Australia 2012

Perth

Monday 6 February
We left England in deep snow. After a mild winter it got cold and the night before we were due to leave it began to snow as we set off for a 50th birthday party. We left at 10:30 and by then the snow was three or four inches deep. I couldn't get through to a taxi firm so we walked; Scharlie in her dancing shoes. But the snow was fine powder and we stayed dry.

The next morning I checked and found our flight had been cancelled. We had that sinking feeling when Trailfinders didn't answer and we resigned ourselves to missing a day. Our first destination was Perth to visit Scharlie's adopted brother Hyung Shik. In desperation we ran him and he contacted Qantas and called back to say we were booked a day later. Scharlie wanted to go to Heathrow but Jon and Richard both said that would be a bad idea. Finally we tried Trailfinders again and they got us on a flight at 9:30pm that night, only an hour later than the flight we had been booked on. Suddenly we had to galvanise ourselves, change gear and finish packing. Jon took us to the station and we made our way to Heathrow and boarded the plane without incident.

We had been dreading the long flight and we had lost our roomy seats because of the cancellation, but in the event it wasn't so bad. After the meal Steve plugged in his earplugs and dozed most of the night. Scharlie couldn't sleep at first and watched films. As we approached Singapore and people were waking she opened a conversation with the man in the window seat and found out that he had been to London for the weekend to see the Leonardo exhibition. This startling admission sparked a lively conversation. He said he was an investment analyst who travelled to Europe once or twice a year. He was courteous soft-spoken and talked intelligently about Australia's economic situation. We parted company in Singapore but he took Steve's card. We planned to stay awake from Singapore to Perth and watch films so we would arrive go to straight bed and sleep. All went well and Hyung Shik and his wife Susan met us looking wide-awake and welcoming and half an hour later, after a drive along the waterfront, we were at their home in Mossman Park. Do you want something to eat? No, but we couldn't resist the sight of a large mango, so we tucked in.

Tuesday 7 February

We woke to bright light in slatted lines from the Venetian blinds. Sue had taken time off work to be with us, and that morning, after breakfast of avocado and tomatoes, peaches, mango and plums we bundled into the car for a tour along the coast as far as Hillarys Marina, some 20 km north of Perth. We had a nice lunch overlooking the ocean and Susan helped Scharlie shop for T-shirts with aboriginal designs for the grandchildren and postcards; Scharlie wants to send the family a postcard trail of our travels. Home in the afternoon a little sick with tiredness and very hot. We had been warned that Perth was experiencing a heat wave of 35°C and it was hot, but again not as difficult to cope with as we expected. Steve went to a shopping centre in Claremont with Hyung Shik and tried to sort out his Internet access. It turned out he needed drivers for his Mac and had to book an appointment for the following day. In the late afternoon we went to Cottesloe, a beautiful white sand beach nearby, with a breakwater built from a natural limestone headland looking out into the Indian Ocean. The sun was losing its strength and the cool water entirely refreshed and made us sweet tempered again. Dinner was under the pergola in the garden, with Sue's amazing cooking and red wine.

Hyung Shik, Susan and Martin's dog Alan, under the pergola

Wednesday 8 February

We made an early start for the Kings Park, a botanical garden with spectacular views of the city centre and the Swan River. The park, around Mount Eliza, is the largest inner city park in the world, two-thirds of which is conserved as bush. It was known as Mooro Katta and was sacred to the Nyoongar people who came there at particular times of the year to hunt kangaroo by herding them up the plateau to the escarpment. Aboriginal people made spears from the jarrah trees growing there and soaked the blossom from marri trees in water to make a sweet drink and ate the seeds and gum. The colonists used convict labour to fell the jarrah trees and red gum marri trees for lumber and quarry the limestone for building stone. The park was rescued from loggers and developers in the late 19th Century by the colony's first surveyor general John Roe and by his successor Malcolm Fraser who persuaded the governor to set aside the land as a public reserve. But the Swan Brewery had built over the aboriginal sacred spring at the foot of Mount Eliza.

It is a beautiful place, part carefully managed with graceful trees and manicured beds and part native bush. It's on a hill, in dramatic juxtaposition to the skyscrapers of the city centre, the so-called city of light. The rich flora and

Perth Central Business District from Kings Park

7

Scharlie examining the Gum trees in Kings park

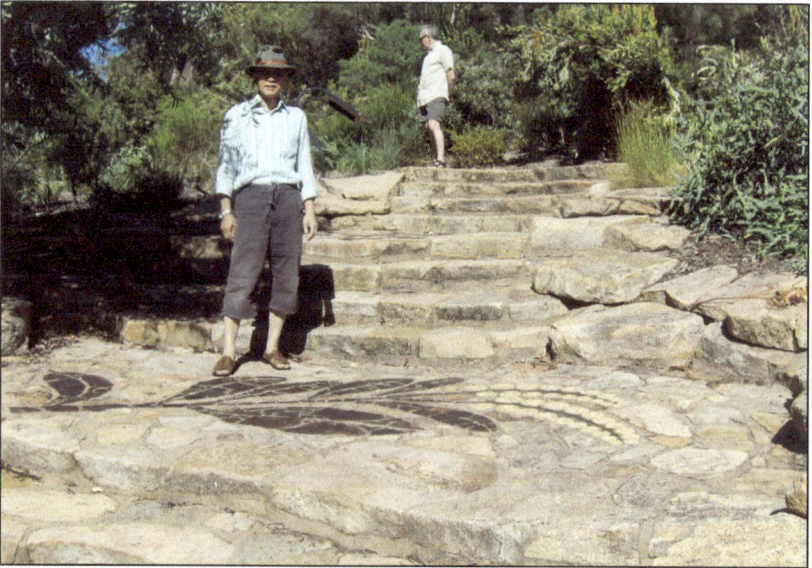

Hyung Shik and patterened stone paving

Gazebo Kings Park

Roof of gazebo

pale white columns of the eucalyptus are set against slender blue/green glass buildings closely clustered around the curve of the bay. The park gave us an immediate insight into Australia – dry sandy soil with soft limestone outcrops densely covered with shrubs and trees capable of reaching a great height. The many varieties of eucalyptus and acacia are labelled with their uses for food, drink, medicine or shelter. Everything was strange and unfamiliar but laid out like a map that could lead you to adventure and understanding.

We wandered around the paths, Scharlie stopping to exclaim about particular plants, and climbed to the top of the double helix tower to get views over Perth. We weren't feeling that well and the climb was a challenge. From there we walked down a grass ride reminiscent of a Chatsworth country park and met Sue for lunch at the Zamia Café a beautiful and popular spot for lunch in the middle of the park. Scharlie, perhaps ill advisedly, had a huge plate of buttermilk muffins with blueberries and cream. Later at home Sue brought out a green eel skin purse and a string of freshwater pearls for Scharlie. You don't come here very often she said.

We went for another swim at a beach where the River Swan narrowed. This is Hyung Shik's favourite spot near the golf course at a little sandy corner that marks the boundary of Mossman Park. As a child, Martinm, their son, used to

High-end architecturural engineering meets Australian bush

come here to fish for blue crab, sadly no more, and Sue and Hyung Shik come to collect mussels on the rocks. This is the way down river to Freemantle and each time a large boat went past it created and mini tsunami. At six we had to leave to have a shower before going to Leah's for dinner.

Sue had stayed home and cooked and we carried the meal in a basket to visit her daughter Leah, husband and new baby. Sue is very organised and clued up about how to get around Perth and deal with the everyday details of life. She is aware that Wednesday is the day you can get cheaper petrol, and saves vouchers for restaurants and ferries. Leah and Wayne live on the other side of Perth. They have a nice house. It's built in the back garden of an old house, a pattern that is popular in this part of town. Leah has taken a year off to look after their new baby, Anneka and Wayne is a dietician working in a hospital giving post-operative advice. While Sue got the meal ready we talked about sharks. He said he wouldn't go swimming at Cottesloe. Four people had been killed this year already, often close to the beach, and had just vanished. The sharks are Great White and Tiger sharks on their migration from India across the ocean and then down the coast following the current south. The great white sharks attack from below. You don't see a thing, said Wayne. I never swim in the sea.

Hyung Shik's favourite spot, where the Swan River narrows at a sandy promontory

The baby is very bonny and Steve got to hold her before Wayne tried to get her off to sleep. On the way back we stopped in the avenue of gum trees in Kings Park to look at the city and the bay in the moonlight. The new camera we bought for the trip seems to take good photos in low light and the pale bark of the eucalyptus looked eerie in the uplighting from lamps sunk into the grass. This is a popular place on a warm clear night like this.

Thursday 9 February

The following morning we went back to King's Park to buy seed of the native plants Scharlie wanted to take back home. Hyung Shik bought us a book on Australia and more postcards for the family. I got one of a Goanna for Malachi. We were very taken by aerial photographs of river systems in Kimberley in the North West. There were lots of beautiful things: jarrah wood boxes, carved seed-like objects and glass and ceramics. From there we went to the city centre and visited the art gallery. They have a number of works by famous aboriginal artists in ochre colours on bark. Most tell stories.

After lunch at home we passed the beach we went to yesterday and skirted the thin sandbank that stretches almost two-thirds of the way across the river.

Kings Park by moonlight

Freemantle, at the mouth of the Swan River, is the port for large ships and there is insufficient depth for any to reach Perth. Sue was waiting. When Hyung Shik and Susan bought their house twenty odd years ago there were large tracts of natural vegetation around them. Now development covers the hills and crowds down to the water's edge from Perth to Freemantle. Yacht clubs abound and the houses crowding the banks are exuberant and individualistic. Each house fills its plot, vying in magnificence with its neighbours.

We swam again at Cottesloe Beach, despite Wayne's warning about sharks. We weren't being reckless; but quick Internet search revealed that only two people had been fatally attacked at Cottesloe since 1990, but one of these was only four months earlier and was fresh in people's minds. We were lucky to see a rehearsal on the sand for tomorrow's opening ceremony of the Perth Festival. An aboriginal man called Barry sang a haunting song to the accompaniment of clashing boomerangs and his mother made a speech, telling the tale of a man and his son. Each day the man had gone out with his shield to fend off the spears thrown at him, she said. The son wanted to go with his father, but his father said he would have to wait till he was a man. The next morning the boy and the shield were missing. The man and his wife ran out, ignoring the spears flying through the air, and found the boy run through

Swimming in the 'shark infested waters' of Cottesloe beach

The boy with his shield fending off the spears thrown at him

The son of the storyteller and a little white girl carried aloft in a white bird

the chest with a spear. The dead boy had spoken to his father and said that his soul was still living. His parents put the boy's soul on the back of a crow, which flew the boy across the ocean to the west. The opening ceremony was at seven the next morning and we vowed to come back.

Steve woke early and lay listening to Cormac McCarthy on his iPhone until it was time to wake Scharlie with a cup of tea and get away quickly without breakfast. Hyung Shik dropped us off and we squeezed between people and found somewhere to sit on the grass terrace in front of the stage. The aboriginal families seemed more nervous than yesterday but the performance was very moving and finished with a procession led by two children, carried aloft in a bamboo sedan chair in the form of a white bird, one the son of the storyteller and the other a little girl descendant of immigrant settlers. On the causeway young men lit 'Black Boys', the Australian grass that grows in the form of a palm and is burned to remove old leaves. Sitting on the grass we had breakfast of fresh fruit Sue had brought, then she set off work and we went to the beach for a last time. There were lots of children in classes learning to swim with instructors. We sunbathed and Hyung Shik took us back for a delicious salmon lunch. We finished the last of the packing and tied bright green ribbons to the suitcases and set off for the airport to fly to Melbourne.

Burning the 'black boys' on the breakwater

Melbourne

Friday 10 February
We are staying with Vicki and Ed, a friend from when we did our doctorates in Cambridge. Our taxi driver found their home in Brighton a suburb on the east side of the bay courtesy of his GPS. We got to bed about eleven after fruit and a glass of wine.

Saturday 11 February
Ed and Vicki took us to their second home at Flinders, a village on the Mornington Peninsula where they rent a house in the country. We drove south through suburbs – bungalow homes and low rise commercial retail buildings until we hit countryside at Arthur's Seat. Ed drove to the top of the 300 m granite bluff to give us a view of the bay. It was sunny but the haze prevented us seeing back to Melbourne clearly. The landscape was green from the recent rains. The impression is English until you look more closely at the trees and realise that they are mainly eucalyptus. There are small vineyards; many with

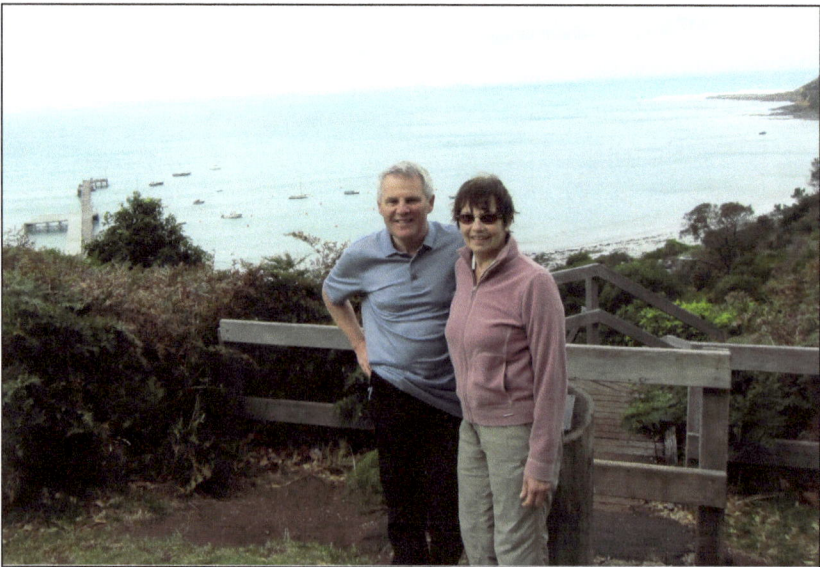

Steve and Scharlie at Mornington Peninsula

restaurants and Ed seemed to know which served good food and wine. The vines are covered with white netting to stop the birds eating the ripening grapes. They'll harvest in the next few weeks.

Vicki had gone ahead and opened the house. It's Edwardian, cream painted timber with large verandas and, we learn later, what's called Federation style. It's not unlike our home in Derbyshire and of the same period. But inside the house is more gracious with high ceilings and mouldings. The floors are highly polished and they have a fireplace. The house was moved here some time ago, most improbably when one considers its size. There are four bedrooms, one with four bunk beds for visiting children, a generous kitchen, living room with sofas and television, and an elegant dining room open to the hallway. They have rented houses in this area for many years and have local friends. Since rents are only 2% of capital value, Ed says, it makes sense to rent. But the owners have planted a lylandii hedge a metre from the veranda with a view to selling half the garden as a building plot, so Ed says they will have to move. They are already looking for somewhere.

We walked into the village – a cross roads with a general store, café and tourist shops and had a light lunch. It's a seaside area rather like the Swan River that the cottages are smaller and set in scrub and trees. Lots of families have

Ed and Vicki's house, Mornington Peninsula

holiday homes here and the village seemed lively but it's difficult to imagine how the shops selling cushions and bric-a-brac survive. We took the papers back to the house. The weather was unsettled and although Scharlie was impatient to go for another walk, Ed persuaded us to wait until it cleared. As we waited for the rain to stop Ed handed us a newspaper and said what did you say was the name of your friend on the plane? There was a large photo of Andrew Sisson. That's him, Scharlie said. The Financial Review featured a story about Andrew's firm being acquired for a huge sum of money by an American company. The article described how he'd out-performed the market, managing a huge fund of $10 billion. It also mentioned that he had started with very little 20 years ago. Ed was impressed. But most interestingly the article went on to say that Andrew had recently donated a work by the Renaissance painter Correggio to the National Gallery where he is a trustee. The painting had been bought at auction at Sotherby's for $5.3m the biggest single donation the gallery had ever received. Even reproduced in the newspaper he painting looked wonderful – a Madonna and Child. We burst out laughing. Why had he been travelling economy class? Scharlie had spent a good part of the night propped up against his back! We had received an email from him just as we were leaving Perth suggesting that we meet in Melbourne and that he'd like

Ed, Vikki and Scharlie on the beach at Mornington Peninsula

to show us some things in the National Gallery. We wondered what we'd say about it when we met.

Finally the skies cleared and we ventured forth, walking down to the beach via steep wooden steps down scrubby tangled cliffs reminiscent of Cornwall. The beach smelt of seaweed and there were white horses on the waves. It felt like England, but the rocks were black and there were many of types of unusual sponge and cuttlefish littering the beach. This is the east side of the peninsula and the waves are from the Bass Strait. There were interesting houses on the headland, some with manicured topiary that Vicki disliked. After half an hour we turned and walked back a different way and with some retracing and looping and good-natured banter between Vicki and Ed, found a new path home across the creek. On the way back Ed drove through Sherborne; a village he came to on holiday as a child. It is actually two separate villages, Old and New Shoreham and people here are very protective of their independence and privileges. The place has changed out of all recognition since Ed was a boy, with new people moving in and building architect designed homes after demolishing the small bungalows. The ones with sea views cost half a million or more. Ed took us past various houses he'd rented in the past.

While Vicki cooked, Ed took us to see kangaroo in a national park called

Expensive looking houses Mornington Peninsula

19

Seawind Garden, near Arthur's Seat. Luckily there was a herd of about 20 just near the car park. Parking the car we moved closer halting each time they looked up quizzically. We crept up slowly, Steve in front with camera at the ready. One or another would raise itself up to monitor his stealthy approach but he got to within 20 yards before they moved off. Moving slowly they use their back legs and tail in a see-saw rocking motion, the tail being used like a fifth leg to balance and take weight while the powerful back legs move forward. As we got closer various animals broke off grazing the short grass and bounded off, hopping with their back legs together. When standing or running their tails lift and curl, their forelegs retract, leaving two small paws visible, and they spring off their hind legs. When grazing they fall forward onto their front legs and the fleshy tail rests on the ground. The garden has been planted like English parkland and, incongruously, a circular rose bed. We got back just before Vicki's friend Georgie arrived. She and her husband are engineers and market a system for detecting vibration in pumps, fans and other rotary machinery. Georgie also runs the women only book club. We talk for most of the meal about books, living down here and about the bits of England.

Kangaroo at Seawind national park

Sunday 12 February

The plan was to visit the Briars nature reserve and Ed asked Steve to check the website and choose a walk. He chose one called Ker-Bur, which meant Koala in the local lingo and the blurb suggested we would see them near the start of the walk.

We chatted to Vicki about her brother and his work on climate change. He is the Australian representative on the climate change panel. He's a zoologist and it turned out that he had authored the book we'd been reading about kangaroo and wallaby. There's a debate about hunting kangaroo. It seems smaller rarer species of marsupial are endangered because of the loss of habitat, rather than the larger species that are hunted. So Vicki's brother argued that the debate should be about what percentage might be culled each year. We didn't see the koala; maybe they were sleeping in the trees at this time of day. It was a pleasant enough walk-through scrub and gum trees.

I asked Vicki what he thought the prospects were for the world agreeing to limit carbon emissions. She said her brother was an eternal optimist. She was less hopeful. She also mentioned that we would be meeting Ed's brother Frank in Melbourne. He's a paediatrician. Earlier in his career he had worked in Papua New Guinea. She described how some years ago a patient had run

Briars nature reserve

amok and started stabbing people. Frank had been severely stabbed and left for dead. At the trial Frank testified that he believed that the attacker had bipolar syndrome and he hadn't been in charge of his actions. I am looking forward to meeting him. Apparently he still can't watch violent films, especially those with knives.

After the walk we climbed the hill to the Homestead and paid 10 dollars for the tour given by a delightful grey-haired lady who kept apologising she was new to the job. The Balcombe family had built the house in the mid-19th century. William Balcombe had been a employee in the East India Company and had been sent to St Helena to manage the company's interest because, she said, he hadn't performed very well. The family hadn't been there very long when Napoleon arrived with his entourage in 1815. Rats overran the house that Napoleon had been assigned, so he was lodged in a pavilion in the Balcombe's garden. For the six years he lived on St Helena Napoleon befriended the Balcombes, especially the youngest daughter Betsy, who from her portrait was a real sweetie. Napoleon loved Josephine, we were told and was very good-looking despite the adverse publicity in the cartoons of the time by Gilray and others. There were a number of dusty rooms with Napoleonic memorabilia including his death mask.

Ker-Bur (Koala) walk; but we didn't see any

Balcombe was hauled back to London and accused of treason for 'assisting Napoleon in corresponding with people in Europe'. The authorities back in England were obviously still paranoid about his possible escape. After all he'd raised an army once before after escaping from Elba and he was only 45 and still vigorous when he was exiled to St Helena. There were drawings of him in shirtsleeves hoeing in the vegetable gardens. But the letters he had posted for Napoleon proved to be personal and of no risk to English interests so Balcombe was exonerated, sent to Victoria as financial secretary to the Treasury and granted 6,700 acres of prime land in the Mornington Peninsula where he had prospered.

We went to the cafe expecting to buy a sandwich and were ushered into a dining room and seated before we could think to object. The host assured us that, despite being short-staffed, we would be served quickly. But the soup and salad took over an hour, so we felt pushed to make our 4 o'clock date at the National Gallery. We had to go home, wash and change and catch the Metro into town. In the event we just caught the train. We got off at Flinders Street, a huge old-fashioned station, and walked over the Yarra River. The gallery is built of sheer slabs of polished dark grey granite. The entrance is through a glass wall entirely covered by a moving film of water and people play photographing

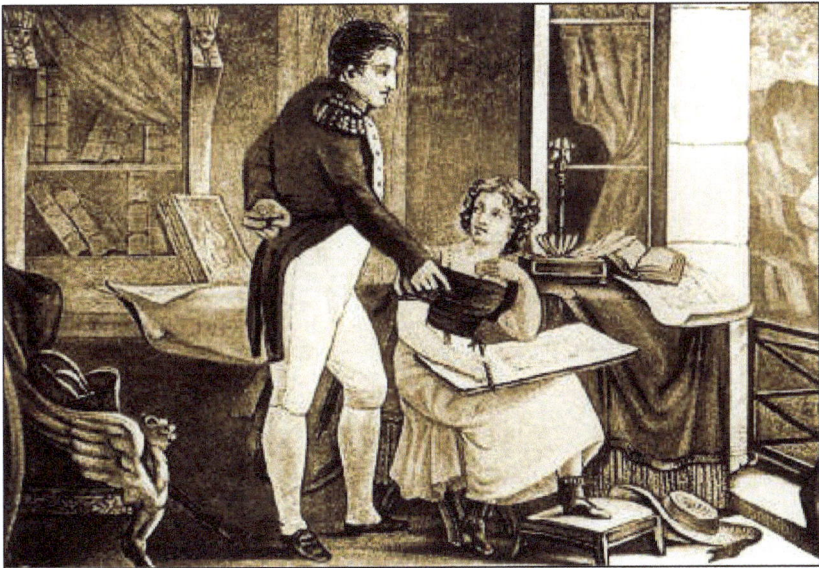

Napoleon and William Balcombe's thirteen year old daughter Betsy on St Helena

themselves through the glass. Andrew asked what we wanted to see and we said we were in his hands. He took as to see the Impressionists and then the Dutch masters. We had only an hour before it closed, which was why we been worried about being late, and time was running out to see the Correggio so we confessed we'd seen an article in the paper that morning. Madonna and Child with the infant Saint John the Baptist was painted by Antonio Allegri, called Correggio, circa 1514-1515.

Andrew exclaimed, Oh no, I have been trying to stall them; the figures were all wrong. Nevertheless, he took us down to see his painting. It is small and exquisite, about 2 foot high by 18 inches wide, in rich reds and greens. The infant Jesus is especially beautiful, with gold curls, his hand resting on John the Baptist's head as if he's about to pull his hair. The detail in the embroidery on Mary's dress and the blue green sheen of her cloak are particularly fine. Andrew pointed out the delicate way in which spikes of gold dust suggested a halo around the Christ child's head. He said that it was extremely rare for a painting of this quality to still be in private hands and to come on the market. He had been lucky that the recession had dulled the appetite of the major European and American galleries and because the Australian currency was strong. The painting will be cleaned and a small crack in the poplar board will

Andrew introducing us to the National Gallery

be repaired. We still had ten minutes so we went up to the second floor to see the watercolours and drawings. We were hustled out at five to five. Clearly donating $5 million cuts no ice or special flavours with staff wanting to get home on time. Hyung Shik had described how people like to start and finish early in Australia and that the longer hours of London workers are unheard of here.

Madonna and Child with infant Saint John the Baptist (c. 1514-1515) Correggio

We wandered up a wide avenue to the shrine to the fallen in the First World War. Andrew said the deaths of so many Australians on the Western front and Gallipoli was etched on the psyche of his parents' generation. His grandfather survived, however, and his father had been a farmer on the Murray River. Andrew came to school in Melbourne and had never left. It's a good place to live, he said. We went on to the Botanic Garden. Andrew had invited us back for tea, but he and Scharlie were fascinated by the garden, especially with a new dry garden built around the reservoir, called the 'volcano', that irrigates the garden and feeds the lakes and is planted with striking prickly cacti from Mexico. He pointed out the bellbirds, which we had heard and thought to be wind chimes, and the 'Black Boy' grasses that grow like ferns in the Australian Lawn section of the garden. We let ourselves out through a small gate on the far side of the garden and reached his house after a short walk.

Scharlie was immediately entranced by a white jasmine in the garden she hadn't seen before. The house nestles between large modern office buildings and is Edwardian Federation style, like Ed and Vicki's house in Flinders, well proportioned with a tile roof and Andrew is obviously proud of it. Inside there were high moulded ceilings, polished hardwood floors, beautiful rugs

New dry garden around 'volcano' reservoir in Botanic Garden, Melbourne

26

and furniture and a spacious and gracious style. Tracy, Andrew's wife, brought in the white wine, olives and a local cheese – a brie from King Island that was very good. All too soon Andrew drove us into town and dropped us just near the restaurant on the South Bank were we had arranged to meet Ed and Vicki. We went in and found Ed's party on the terrace. We realised we'd left our camera in Andrew's car so after he had dropped us we texted him and, most kindly, he drove back with it.

Over dinner we had a long talk with Frank, Ed's brother, about some research on immunology he had been asked to review. Using anthropological methods, the author had been able to demonstrate that in many malnourished populations the order in which inoculations are given is critical to mortality rates. The medical community is having difficulty digesting the findings because the author isn't a medic. Frank is a paediatrician with irrepressible energy who goes on desert expedition each year working for WHO pioneering inoculation of African children. John, Ed's cousin, is a lawyer working for profit charities. John's wife said she was born in India and had a business commissioning designer clothing to be made in different parts of India. She described the prejudice she'd experienced when she told people she had been born in Calcutta. The meal was very good and we were enjoying talking but again we

Andrew and Tracey's home in the centre of Melbourne

had to leave and it didn't occur to us to say we would get a later train.

Monday 13 February

We had a late start as Scharlie was showing Vicki how to prune, so it wasn't until lunchtime that we went into Brighton to a bookshop to get presents. The prices seemed astronomical and we spent a lot on books. Vicki drove us into and dropped us near Andrew's house so we could go to the parts of the Botanic Garden we missed yesterday. We walked through the fern gully and then over to the observatory for a drink in a café. We found our way to the Arts Centre and asked for the Australian Gallery, but it was closed on Mondays. So we went, round the National Gallery again. We looked at the 20th-century stuff on the top floor but we weren't impressed and we went to look at the Correggio again – it's very fine. From the gallery we walked along Flinders Street past the railway station to the Immigration Museum. Inside they had recreated cabins on a sailing clipper and passenger liner. Scharlie had the sensation we were rolling with the sound of the swell and engine noise

Dinner with Ed's family

and was convinced she was getting seasick. Interestingly she was worse in the passenger liner because of the engine noise. The power of association! Some of the personal histories of early migrants were very moving.

Finally we left to catch a train on the circular loop around the business district. The tram was an old wooden vehicle driven with a large brass wheel. We had to stop at every junction and the trip took much longer than we thought. We went down to the old docks where they are building apartment blocks and passed the Parliament House, the Cathedral and the jail were Ned Kelly was imprisoned. So we saw a little bit of the town.

Luckily we just caught a train as it was leaving and got back home in good time. Vicki had chosen a fish restaurant five minutes from where Andrew lived and Ed drove us in. Andrew said they'd also driven because Tracy was in heels. They were already seated. Andrew was in suit and tie. Ed had clued us into the dress code here and Steve was wearing a dark jacket. Most gratifyingly everyone was relaxed. Ed and Andrew hit it off and talked about the economic climate, rather than their own work. Tracey and Vicki found they had done the same course in economics and politics, although a year apart, at Monash University. Tracy said that Andrew was tied to the company for five years, but wanted to study art history.

Glass wall in National Gallery

Scharlie was restless so she stayed up till midnight and read, which seem to work as she had a good night sleep. Vicki's driver Antonio arrived at 9.30 and drove us along the coastal promenade; runners and cyclists taking their morning exercise still, and through St Kilda's where Vicki used to live. You can't walk on the beach without shoes any more, said Antonio, because of the needles. We said we liked the new townhouses we passed, but our driver thought they stifled Australian individuality and freedom. You can paint your front door the colour you want but that's it. People need their own bit of garden, he said, pointing to some chaotic bungalow houses we were passing.

We bought more T-shirts at the airport – we are flying to Christchurch; only Tom, Jess and Maddie to buy for still. They didn't serve food on the flight so we bought a couple of frittatas to put us on!

Queen Elizabeth and Sydney Harbour Bridge

Sydney

29 February

From the airport we got the Metro into town and caught a glimpse of the Harbour Bridge, the Opera house and the Queen Elizabeth cruise ship. Getting off the train everyone flowed onto the escalator and we followed. But Steve's heavy case tipped over and knocked him off his feet head down. Steve scrabbled with his hands to stop sliding down until someone shouted to turn it off and someone found the emergency button. Steve sat on the cold steps of the escalator and composed himself. The stationmaster arrived asked if he was okay. Steve asked if he had any first aid and, taking us to his office, he sprayed Steve's torn leg and elbow with antiseptic. You'll feel it tomorrow, he said as we filled in his accident form. The leg was already swelling but Steve could walk and the damage wasn't that bad and luckily he hadn't cut his trousers or bashed his face.

The Swiss hotel was much more luxurious than the Comfort hotel in Wellington. A bellboy brought our luggage up and showed us how to work

Sydney Harbour Bridge

the room. The tea things were in a fitted cabinet with a mini-bar and I thought he said the bar was courtesy of the hotel. I rang reception to check and then regretted it when they asked me if he was a young German. I said I didn't want to get him in trouble. We'd had lots to eat on the plane so we weren't hungry, and since it wasn't that late we went for a walk. We'd had lots to eat on the plane so we weren't hungry, and since it wasn't that late we decided to go for a walk. We were on the 12th floor and getting to the street involved going to the lobby on the eighth floor and getting a second elevator to the street. The bellboy glared at us on our way out. We walked down George Street to the harbour. It began raining and we walked along the quay admiring the Queen Elizabeth docked there till tomorrow at midnight. It was raining and we were tired so we caught the Metro back and went to bed. We'd spotted a restaurant on the quayside called Wolfies and had taken a card. Later we rang and booked for the following evening.

Steve got up early and went to the Apple Store at 8am when it opened and had managed to change his laptop battery. He was worried because hadn't finished preparing the lecture he had to give next week in Tsinghua University Beijing. They fitted him in without a problem and changed it under the three-year warranty. We found a swanky restaurant to have muesli and

Sydney Opera House

fruit for breakfast in the elegant arcade of Queen Victoria Building. It seems it's a meeting place for businessmen with briefcases, smiles and handshaking and lovers waiting and then greeting each other with kisses and hugs.

Sydney in the rain –now we're glad we have our macs. But the rain is warm and the wet pavement splashes pleasantly on our sandaled feet. Our plan is to visit the Museum of Australia, then a walk through the Botanic Gardens to the National Gallery. We walk through Hyde Park and are lucky; there is an exhibition of aboriginal paintings based on the Canning Stock Trail – the thousand mile cattle drive from Kimberley in the North through the desert to the gold fields. The guide explained that exhibition was the result of a cooperative effort between the tribes that live in the area along the drovers' road. We want to tell our story, to get it out there, he said. The aborigine tradition is an oral one our history is learned and captured in ritual dance and song. History is not about time passing it's about place – about the emotion of particular experiences that happened in a particular place, for example being bitten by a dog or a murder; its about the geology and the shape of the land and all the food that can be found there and, above all, the waterholes. The ancients had rock paintings but until recently the stories of the dreaming were learned through drawings in the sand which were wiped away when

Queen Victoria Building, Sydney

Kulilli *by Wimmitji Tjapangarti, Warlayirti Artists, 1990, describing story of ancestral Tingari men and kipara (bush turkey) man and his family who travelled east of Canning Stock Route*

the ceremonies were over and singing and dancing were part of communal learning. The building of the drovers' road was a disaster for the people many of whom had never seen white men before. The water holes were turned into deep inaccessible wells or polluted by horses and cattle.

Canning discovered the whereabouts of the water holes that made the Stock Trail possible by capturing Aborigines and chaining them together and giving them salt water to drink so when he released them they made straight for the waterhole. Women were raped and men killed. The aboriginal went to the road to spear bullocks. The drive, which crosses the Rabbit Proof fence, was only in operation 20 years as the drovers found the route too dangerous. Even punitive raids by police columns sent from Perth failed to stop the many spearings. Gradually people were gathered to live in missions where they received Western food and medicine and their ceremonies were frowned upon. Many families were separated and now, many years later, the Canning Road project has traced people who had lived along the great length of road but had been dispersed.

We were very taken by the art and went round a second time with an aboriginal guide who explained the significance of place rather than time in aboriginal culture and oral history and how the various tribes intermarried

Dream of the emu

Mangarri (food) *by Elizabeth Nyumi, Warlayirti Artists, 2007, showing the abundant bush tucker = munyunpa (plum bush), lungki (whitchetty grubs) and walku (quandong).*

and passed complex knowledge about survival in this harsh environment through their songs. He drew many comparisons between the marriage customs and economy of aboriginal culture and what he regarded as the errors of the West.

They were invited to go back to the country where they were born and remember their history in paint. Many were painted collaboratively by a group during ceremonial dancing and singing. As well as the paintings there were videos of people telling their life stories and groups revisiting their homeland and initiating their children in the old ways. Whereas early bark painting used natural pigments, these artists had access to acrylic colour and their choice a combination of colour works is exquisite; oranges and reds were dominant but many shades were subtly used. Like impressionist paintings the patterns come alive at a distance and the colours changed with the angle of light.

Having spent some time looking at the paintings ourselves we were invited in by aboriginal guide who had been brought up on a mission. He was a passionate advocate for his people and a fierce critic of colonisation. He thought capitalism was all about selfish greed, while aboriginal ceremony and dreaming was to help people to live with each other without conflict. Before the white man came the aboriginal lifestyle was healthy, bush tucker was good,

Dream of the kangaroo

and life had meaning that had nothing to do with property or acquisition of wealth. Aboriginal artists are thriving now but you don't hear much about Aboriginals in other fields. We sat on the floor in the main foyer right at the front and were enthralled by a performance of Aboriginal song and dance. There was one main singer and storyteller, who explained how different people had bequeathed or given him permission to sing their songs, two didgeridoo players and two dancers who danced and sang the dream of the kangaroo, emu and snake. The sound of the instruments and the movement of the dancers astonishing.

We spent a while here and stopped for lunch, a huge carton of lentils and quiche, in the museum cafe. We leave reluctantly, five hours later, wiser and with our heads filled with colour and stories, dance and song. It was raining and we walked over to the Art Gallery of NSW to look at more art from northern Queensland and Arnhem Land and compared early Aboriginal bark paintings with 19th-century colonial paintings. One painting portrayed the aborigines as noble savages living in an unspoilt world before Europeans. By the time we got out it was dusk and raining hard. We were tired so we walked back to the hotel rather than going on to the Botanic Garden and the opera house. We were to regret our decision bitterly the next morning.

Rainy day leaving National Galley, Sydney

It was windy that evening and at Wolfies we were seated on the road side next to a plastic curtain that let in cold drafts of air, but the atmosphere was good, our Chinese waiter kind and attentive, the food excellent and we had a good evening. After the meal we wandered down the quay and up onto a viewing platform to see the great liner and speculated about where it might be going on to at midnight. We could see the light of Sydney Harbour Bridge and the Opera House silhouetted across the Bay, but this was the nearest we got to them, since we discovered that our plane left in the morning rather than the evening as Steve had thought. We hauled the luggage through the elegant Queen Victoria Building and caught the Metro to the airport – disappointed that our plans for a ferry trip to the zoo and a tour of the Opera House were not to be. We had even been talking about a trip to the Blue Mountains. Next stop Shanghai.

Dinner at Wolfies restaurant

Australia from the air